Run A Risk Workshop Learn by Shadowing

Pierre Kouhozon

Copyright © 2019 Pierre Kouhozon

All rights reserved.

ISBN: 9781798150795

CONTENTS

SECTION 1: THE SCENARIO V
SECTION 2: ANNEXES 57
Annex 1 – Risks Management Plan 58
Annex 2 – Risks monitoring 69

BIBLIOGRAPHY AND INTERNET REFERENCES 71

Projects 71
Anecdotes 71

Section 1: The scenario ...

PROLOGUE

AssurTGE is a company specializing in the insurance of very large companies.

It has established itself in European countries through twenty-seven subsidiaries. Christophe Proudy, 55 years old, graying hair, is the current CEO (Chief Executive Officer). Each subsidiary develops and runs its agencies' network. In France, the network has fifty agencies. To expand its activities, the multinational insurance Globalinrance acquires it in August 2020.

Historically, each subsidiary uses its local management software in its network. The softwares are interfaced with other tools in accounting, corporate finance, market finance, procurement, and logistics. Some modules of market finance and logistics are accessible from mobile terminals.

As part of a program designed to standardize the group's information system, AssurTGE launches the project "AlphaProject" that will provide a new centralized management software called "Centragiciel". This software will help to manage the flow of information between all affiliates.

The project started two years ago. The deadlines were communicated to all subsidiaries. But the implementation is not going as planned: the schedule of the intermediate deliveries slip endlessly, the budget is not under control anymore, the quality of the deliveries is below expectations, the team's morale is affected, the directors of the subsidiaries have lost hope and no longer believe in the success of the project. Christophe Proudy then hires a professional project manager to get the project back on track.

As part of his activities to reschedule the project, Alan brings together the stakeholder representatives for a risk management workshop.

Esin, Gama, Delly, Zely, Ethan, Alfan and Betty represent the Research and Development (R & D) department in their respective areas of expertise.

Figure 1 shows the AssurTGE organization chart.

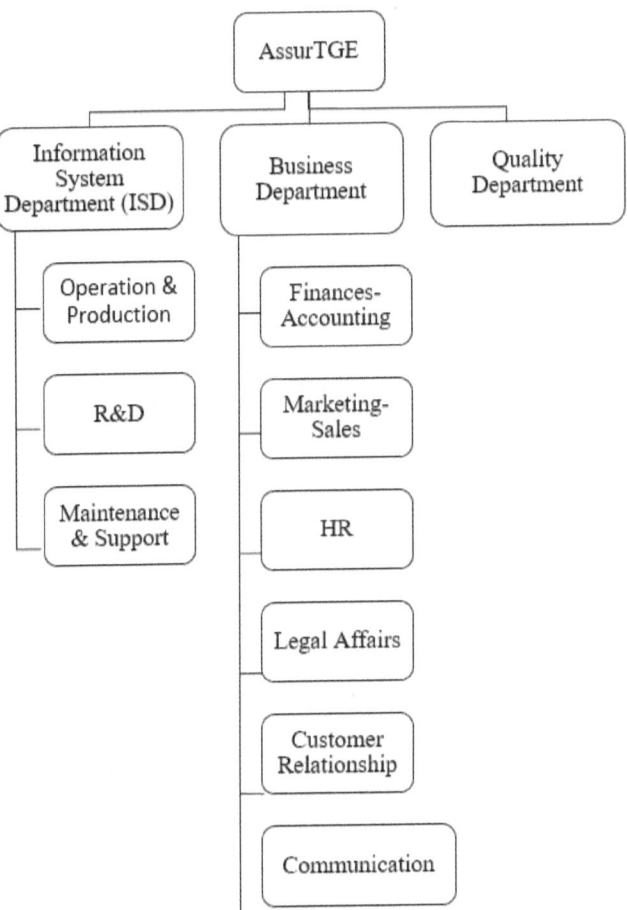

Figure 1. AssurTGE organization chart

PIERRE KOUHOZON

1

To prepare the workshop on the risks, Alan connects to the shared server where information and data from all projects are stored. He goes through the files looking for a list of risks or problems that occurred during past projects. *I would have been surprised to find one.* To be sure, he asks his line manager and the Quality Director and they confirm the result of his research: no historical data on risks from past projects. Then, he opens a blank document, prepares a table with the following headers: No., Title, Description, Probability, Impact, Severity, Cost of Risk, Mitigation plan, Owner. He named it "AlphaProject-RiskRegister", takes his computer and goes to the meeting room where all the people he has invited are waiting for him.

"So, let's go!" he says, in a motivated tone. "Today, we're going to address the risks. But first, we need to agree on what I mean by 'risk'."

"Good idea," a participant adds, "it makes sure we talk about the same thing."

"Exactly!" Alan confirms.

"OK," he continues, "I'll refer to the definition given by a world-known project management professional organization. It's called 'Project Management Institute' or PMI. Moreover, for those interested, it has published a book on methodology, processes and tools on project management, and updates it regularly. This book, known as pmbok, is considered the 'bible of project management' in the project management world. Better, it offers certifications for those who are willing to professionalize in project management."

"Oh, yes? Not bad!" Esin interrupts. "What is their website? I'd like to know more about those certifications."

"Simply pmi.org for the US site and pmi-france.org for France. I really recommend to those who are attracted by project management to take at least one of the certifications. It restructures the brain and can significantly boost your career."

"Me," Gama says jokingly, "the PMI I know in France is 'Protection Maternelle et Infantile' which literally means 'Maternal and Infant Protection'".

A burst of laughter in the room.

"OK," Alan resumes, laughing, "let's go back to our definition of risk. 'A project risk is an uncertain event or condition that, if it occurs, has a positive or negative effect on one or more project objectives such as scope, schedule, cost and quality'".

"Positive effect?" someone asks spontaneously.

RUN A RISK WORKSHOP: LEARN BY SHADOWING

"Yes! When the effect is positive, it's called 'opportunity' and when it's negative, it's called 'threat'. It will be clearer later, you'll see!"

"Hum," Gama says. "I can see what you're getting at. When you think about it, it makes sense. We are so used to trying to avoid threats, and we forget that we can also act on opportunities to achieve our desires. Normal! It's our primary survival instinct. But there're also opportunities in our everyday life: you just need to know how to open wide your mind to recognize them and not miss them.

"Absolutely!" Delly adds. "I totally agree with Gama. Sometimes even things that seem like a threat are an opportunity when you dig a little; this happens often to me. I only take a step back, think quickly and by magic, the threat turns into an opportunity. But, for that to work, you must first have in mind a clear objective. That is the starting point!"

The participants comment on Delly's remark and start telling each other about the opportunities they have had in their life.

"OK, OK, OK," Alan says. "Let's go back to our main subject of the moment after this short philosophical digression. The second point of alignment: how to formulate risks?"

He pauses briefly before resuming as if to let the group try to answer.

"It's very simple; all you need is to make sure the following elements appear in its description:"

- ✓ The cause, ie the situation that causes the risk
- ✓ The event, ie the threat or likely opportunity
- ✓ The impact on the project objectives

"Uh ... Can you give an example?" Delly asks, confused.

"Of course!"

Alan goes to the board then writes and reads at the same time: "Delay in receiving the AXM software license that could postpone the start of the management module integration leading to deliver Centragiciel v1 late."

"I let you read and find in this description the cause, the event, and the impact."

He pauses again to give the time to the participants to think.

"OK, I've got it!" Delly says. "So, in your example, the cause is the delay in receiving the license, the event is to postpone the integration of the module 'management', and the impact on the project objectives is the delay of Centragiciel v1 delivery."

"Exactly!"

"Well, this type of delay is also possible for materials we need in the project. So, should we consider them as risks as well?" Delly asks.

"Yes!" Alan responds. "However, the probabilities that they occur might be different or the impacts might not be the same. That's why It's necessary to specify separately the risks per external deliverable. This helps to better follow them. Another example: There's also that difficulty often encountered to obtain clarifications on certain business requirements while they are being developed."

Alan opens his document "AlphaProject-RiskRegister" and notes in the column "Description" as they formulate the risks.

"Of course," he continues, "even if the requirements have been already validated, developers could need business expertise throughout the project for clarification and possible adjustments. For this risk, we can mention: 'Inadequate support of business which can delay the understanding of certain requirements and lead to their redevelopment.'"

"OK, it's clear!" Gama says. "The cause is the lack or insufficiency of business support; the event is the misunderstanding of certain requirements and the impact is to rework what is already done."

"Personally, I can see a technical risk on performance," Esin says. "Given the growing number of the module 'management' users, our servers might be overloaded."

"OK, we're almost there! Let's do it together with a question and answer," Alan suggests.

"What is the cause?"

"The growing number of the module 'management' users," answers Esin.

"What is the potential threat from it?"

"The servers that host Centragiciel may be overloaded with simultaneous connections," Esin says again.

"What will be the impact on the project if that dreaded threat occurs?"

"Users won't be able to access Centragiciel," Gama answers.

"In other words," Esin says, "it gives us something like: 'The growing number of the module 'management' users that could lead to server overload and prevent users to access Centragiciel.'"

"Perfect! I note that too," Alan says.

"But so far, no opportunity has been mentioned; can we really find one on a project like this?" Esin asks.

"I do see one," Zely says: "'Renegotiation of pricing conditions with our provider People2YourC that could lower the current daily rate and reduce the team cost.'"

"Here is another similar," Alan adds: "'Negotiation ongoing to hire an expert that will work on the billing module to make its evolutions and parameterization more efficient.'"

"Yeah, it will be cool if this expert joins us. But, isn't sure he's hired?" Zely asks.

"No… because of the contractual constraints between AssurTGE and the publisher. But there's a one-in-two chance he joins us during the project."

Together they list many risks and very quickly run out of ideas.

"In fact, now that we've understood how to formulate the risks, the most complicated is to identify them, I think," one of the participants in the group says. Any trick for that?"

"OK, here's how we will proceed," Alan responds. "We will play a project 'pre-mortem' game. We'll focus on the 'fishing for threats'".

Alan takes a sip and continues. The group listens religiously, curious to discover the technique he is going to propose.

"You will imagine that you're in the future, the project is completed but failed. You then meet to determine the reasons for the failure. To find these reasons, imagine that you're on the project, each fulfilling his role. Then, again with your imagination, scroll through the project execution from the beginning to the final delivery, even until the moment you received the first user's feedbacks. Proceed step by step, and write down all the events that come to your mind."

He thinks for a moment looking for how to better explain his thought, then repeats:

"Well! Let me say it differently. You are in the future at the end of this failed project. With your imagination, you are visualizing the film of the progress of the project, phase by phase, from beginning to end. Each time, you capture an event that negatively impacts the project scope, its budget, or its deadline, or the quality of what is delivered or all of the above."

"Hold on!" Ethan interrupts him. "By 'phase by phase' you mean 'definition of needs', 'specification', 'design', 'development', etc.?"

"Exactly!"

"Oh yeah …" Ethan exclaims. "That's right; it must be fun to visualize the project scenes like a movie! But there, we have to get very creative. Anyway, let's try!"

"Yes," Alan says. "Visualize is the key!"

"You each have five minutes to imagine the list of reasons why the project failed," he continues. "Then, in turn, everyone will read an idea from his list and write it on the board. Then, you'll start again the roundtable until exhausting your lists."

"Obviously," another person interrupts him, "we'll likely have a problem with the formulation of the risks, no? We have little time to imagine the ideas. As we aren't experts in risk formulation, it's not going to be short? We will end up wanting to capture ideas quickly and at the same time, formulate them as you ask. I'm afraid it disturbs us and slow us down!"

"You've done well to notice this point," Alan responds. "We will do step by step. Just focus on catching ideas and write them down as you wish. We will formulate the corresponding risks afterward. Of course, this does not prevent those who feel comfortable in formulating the risks of doing it at the same time as they capture their ideas!"

"Can we start? Is that clear?" he asks.

Silence.

"OK," Alan says. "This could help you. What are the areas in which we can encounter problems?"

Participants cite untidily the areas and he writes them down on the board, repeating them aloud. In that way, the group progressively develops the list below. He finishes writing them and immediately goes back to his computer to take notes.

- ✓ Project scope
- ✓ Technology
- ✓ Quality
- ✓ Resources
- ✓ Communication
- ✓ Supplier
- ✓ Dependency between modules
- ✓ Dependence on other projects
- ✓ Stakeholder involvement

"Hmm, what are these categories for?" a participant asks.

"Threats could come from many sources," Zely replies. "Knowing the possible sources will help us find them quickly; they guide us. Is that the idea behind?"

"That's exactly the point!" Alan confirms. "But, be careful! Every time, write down all the ideas that cross your mind without trying to limit yourself to a given category."

"Well, I'm repeating myself again to get you back into it," he continues. "Imagine yourself in the future. The project ended bad! Yes, very bad! It messed up. Centragiciel is delivered several months late. It's unusable! The team is exhausted and only looking for one thing: get out of the project quickly and do not repeat such an experience! In short, let's say it's a disaster. We will start with the category 'project scope'. Try to imagine the events related to the project scope that led to such a failure. Give free rein to your imagination; do not repress any idea that crosses your mind. Think about requirement gathering, definition, specification, development, etc."

"So, can we start?" Alan asks again.

The group agrees. The room is immersed in silence. Alan doesn't speak anymore. After a few minutes, he says: "Remember the rules. In three minutes, everyone will share their ideas with the group." Still a deep silence. After five minutes, he marks the end: "Stop, time is over!" All participants start talking to each other at the same time in a hubbub.

Alan waits a few minutes for the room to be quiet again.

"So, could you come up with ideas? Who wants to share one of his ideas first?" Alan asks.

"It's really hard your exercise," a participant responds. "focused as I might be, I haven't found any idea. In fact, I don't even know where to begin."

All the participants start talking again at the same time, causing even more noise than before. Some say, "Yes, it's the same!" Others "I confirm, really hard!"

"OK… quiet please…" Alan says loudly enough to be heard. "That's normal; it's the beginning. It will be easier afterward by practicing."

Silence.

"Let me give you an example. Suppose we delivered Centragiciel, and users find that more than half of the features they were expecting missed. One can imagine an event having a negative consequence on the scope as: 'The end users are not involved during the gathering of the needs and therefore the functional requirements cover only part of their needs'. There, do you agree that we can say there is a reason for the project failure?"

Some participants say, "Oh, yes, all right," others say, "Well done!" One adds more loudly to be heard by all: "Ah, I agree, if we forget half the work, it's not cool! Failure is certain!"

"Well, here we go. We'll start again with the category 'Scope'. Remember, look no further. Do not repress any idea that crosses your mind, write them down on paper!"

He gives the starting signal. The room is quiet again. Total calm. No participant writes. Alan worries and wonders if they will succeed in finding ideas this time. To occupy the time that seems long, he gets up, walks to the door, opens it quietly to make no noise, takes a look in the hallway as if looking for someone, carefully closes the door and returns to his place. When he returns, all the participants are writing something on their notebook or laptop for some. After five minutes, Alan says, it's time to stop.

Again, discussion among participants for a short while.

"So, is it a little simpler this time? Who shares one of his ideas first?" he asks.

A participant proposes to start, goes to the board, and writes while reading: 'All business areas are not represented during the workshop on definition of need and therefore many necessary and useful features were missing'. Proud of the list of ideas he could find, he was going to move on a second when Alan stops him.

"Great! Thank you," Alan says. "Now, let's continue with the person on your left. We will go around the table. You will take turns until you exhaust your list in the current category."

The next person stands up and mentions: 'The business representatives were not available to see the product intermediate stages while developers were building it to adjust it if necessary.'

Participants exhaust their ideas for the category 'Scope'. Alan suggests they take a short break before continuing with the following areas.

After the break, they continue with the category 'Technique'.

"OK, here we go again. Can you see what could have happened technique-wise on that crazy project?" Alan says.

A developer says, laughing: "Ah ... technique! If they could listen to us ...". Alan also laughs: "This is actually the time to listen to you!"

Five minutes later, a developer suggests: "We discover very late that many SQL commands used in stored procedures are not compatible with our database management system version."

A second says: "We discover very late that the codes of some modules are so complex that it's very difficult or impossible to modify them".

A third adds: "The number of interfaces appears high and made the architecture too complex. So, any modification or correction requires a disproportionate workload."

"Wow! You've found many ideas in this area," Alan says surprised.

"Yes, the machine 'Imagination' is now launched," replies a participant, happy.

"So, let's move on to the next category," Alan says.

The group proceeds that way, category by category and produces a long list which extract is below:

Scope

- ✓ End users are not involved in requirements collection and therefore the functional requirements only cover part of their needs.
- ✓ All business areas are not represented during the definition of the need and therefore many necessary and useful features were missing from the final product.

- ✓ Business representatives were not available to see the intermediate steps of the product as it was built to adjust it if necessary.
- ✓ Many functional features not required by business are developed at the initiative of the developers.
- ✓ Many non-functional requirements are missed during requirements definition.

Technical

- ✓ We discover very late that many SQL commands used in stored procedures are not compatible with the version of our database management system.
- ✓ We discover very late that the codes of some modules are so complex that it's very difficult or impossible to modify them unless they're completely redeveloped.
- ✓ The number of interfaces appears high and made the architecture too complex. So, any modification or correction requires a disproportionate workload.
- ✓ It was discovered very late that the interface between module X and module Y causes a bottleneck that affects performance.
- ✓ The server that host the sources of some modules crashed whereas there are no recent backups.
- ✓ As delivery approaches, a developer mistakenly removes a class shared by all modules, causing a bug whose cause is very hard to find.

Quality

- ✓ The business representatives are not involved in the validation of the test plan and therefore many

use cases cause critical anomalies not detected during the validation but only encountered later in production.
- ✓ We realize very late that Centragiciel overloads quickly in many scenarios of use.
- ✓ A change is made at the last minute and causes regressions that take weeks to fix.
- ✓ A fix considered "minor" is delivered quickly without being validated by the validation team in order to save time and cause a critical anomaly.

Resource

- ✓ Some experts are not available to support the team
- ✓ Many developers who work on critical activities are often solicited on other projects and therefore are not focused on their activities.
- ✓ Inexperienced developers are positioned on complicated tasks without training on technology and therefore consume a lot of senior developers' time.
- ✓ There is no budget anymore to extend certain contractor's contract on the project.
- ✓ The atmosphere is tense in the team and they make many mistakes or rush through their work.

Provider

- ✓ Late delivery of suppliers (licenses, external software components and hardware)
- ✓ Delay in the development of the internal component CC causing a delay in the delivery of Centragiciel.

Other

- ✓ Many project activities are forgotten and the project time and budget are underestimated.
- ✓ The project manager wrongly estimated a lot of activities and therefore the project time and budget are underestimated.

Alan pauses for a moment, looks around the room and continues:

"Be careful! Do not go so fast on this list. Review it! Take a few minutes to think and see if you have any other risk ideas. It's the basis of the next step of our risk analysis."

PIERRE KOUHOZON

2

"Now," Alan begins, "let's come back to the present moment. Get back in our project's context. We will retain the ideas that are really applicable to AlphaProject."

"Oh yes, we must," Alfan adds. "I've really thrown out all the possible bad things that could happen during a project; not sure they're all applicable in our context."

The group goes through the list of ideas together and marks "NA" in front of those he thinks to be too imaginary and cannot apply to AlphaProject. Alan displays only the list of selected ideas.

"OK," Alan resumes, "it's time to deduce the risks. We will reword them together so that they are easy to understand. Do you remember our famous 'Cause / Event / Impact' model?"

"Of course," one participant says, "this is not going to take long, now that we have got the ideas. It's just a question of rewording."

"Um," Alan says. "For some ideas, that's correct. But we'll probably fall on others where it will be necessary for example to ask the question like: 'why the event could happen?'"

Alan projects on the screen the document "AlphaProject-RiskRegister" that contains the list of risks they had already registered. He keeps open the document that contains the ideas and continues.

"Well, if you take the idea 'end users are not involved in the gathering of needs and therefore the functional requirements only cover part of their needs', the risk can be quickly formulated. Any proposal?"

Alfan starts:

"Something like ...: 'Non-involvement of end users, which may cause an incomplete definition of the need, leading to the redevelopment of Centragiciel.'"

"That's it!"

A participant reacts:

"Uh ... I'd have rather said it another way ... 'Non-involvement of end users, which might cause an incomplete definition of need, leading to rework'."

"Isn't that the same?" another participant replies. "I could turn it to you in many different ways too!"

"Yes, of course, that's okay too!" Alan answers. "The key is to bring out the 'probable causes/event/impacts' and express the risk in a simple way so that it's understood."

Alan gets up, goes to the board, turns to the screen where the list of ideas is displayed and continues.

"But, if you take this one..."

He writes while reading: "We discover very late that many SQL orders used in stored procedures are not compatible with our database management system version."

"It will need a little extra effort to deduce the risk, I think. Someone wants to try?" he asks.

Some participants all together begin laughing: "Well, who has proposed this complicated idea?"

"Don't laugh, guys," one of them intervenes. "We often face this problem! And I've never seen anyone anticipate it. We do well to mention it here."

His colleagues continue laughing and say, "Ah, you are the culprit; we're waiting for your formulation".

Suddenly, Alfan interrupts and turns himself in:

"No! He is not! I did propose this idea. In the context of AlphaProject, here is what I meant: 'Insufficient knowledge of the specificities of the DBMS in the team which might result in writing incompatible SQL commands leading to redevelop them.'"

"Perfect!" Alan resumes. "Before we start to take them in the order, let's look at this one: 'We discover very late that the codes of some modules are so complex that it's very difficult or impossible to modify them unless redeveloped completely'. It could give: 'Lack of inspection of legacy codes before the estimate of developments which may result in redeveloping some modules and increase project costs and time'. Couldn't it?"

The team goes through the ideas one after the other. Alan writes the descriptions in the risk register. It's 12:10 am, the risk identification is complete. Alan suggests that participants go to lunch and back at 1:30 pm to continue.

Some go to the canteen to have lunch together. Sitting around a circular table, they tell each other their evening of the day before, their last film and the last book they read. Ethan, staring at his smartphone, burst out laughing and begins to tell his story out loud so that all his colleagues can hear. They listen to him all, calmly.

"According to the scientists," he starts, "two black holes have collided and this would have caused waves in the Universe."

"Hmm ... black hole. What's that, again?" Delly asks.

"These are super-dense celestial objects, or compact ones if you want, that attract and trap any matter or light that passes near them," Ethan answers. "They are impressive, even the light can't escape their force of attraction."

All his colleagues listen attentively, eager to know more about the story.

"The two which collided," he continues, "would be eight or fourteen times as great as our star, the Sun. Astronomical numbers, you might say, when you know that we're speaking about billions of billions of billions of tons just for the Sun's mass."

With a very skillful movement, he wraps around his fork a portion of the succulent spaghetti carbonara on his plate, swallows it and accompanies it with a sip of sparkling water.

"Imagine the scene," he continues, accompanying his description with the movements of his hands, focused as if he was watching a movie. "Two huge stars wander in space, each one rotating around each other. Suddenly, they head towards each other at a crazy speed of about 150 000 km / h while continuing to turn one around the other, come closer by describing spirals increasingly tight, and in a split second, boom ... collide! They then merge into a gigantic black hole of about twenty times the sun's mass. Twenty times! Huge! The impact vibrates the whole space as predicted by the physicist Albert Einstein just a century ago. Massive ripples begin to spread in space like waves caused by a stone thrown into a lake."

"Wow!" exclaims one of the colleagues. "It was these waves that were detected on Earth only on September 14, 2015?"

"Exactly," Ethan responds. "They spread to us and could be detected for about a second with sophisticated instruments. Scientists call these ripples gravitational waves. The most surprising thing is that, according to the scientists, this collision occurred 1.4 billion light years from Earth. These waves traveled for more than a billion years before reaching us."

"More than a billion years? Unbelievable!" Delly says. "What a beautiful trip in a so distant past! But hey, we have to finish eating fast and come down to Earth. It's time to get back to work."

It's 1:30 pm, the workshop resumes.

"Now, it's time to analyze our risks," Alan begins.

"Uh ... Analyze the risks!?" Delly exclaims. "Are you sure we're the right persons for that? I am not sure we know much about it. Well ... not me anyway!"

"You will see," Alan continues, "this part will be simpler than the definition of the risks. Remember, the events we have described are uncertain. During the course of our project, they could occur but they could also not happen. Right? Well, you have now the privilege to say what the probabilities for them to occur are."

"A probability to occur?" one of the participants asks. "We must be soothsayer to answer that, no? For example, we will say that the probability of an event A to occur is 60% or the one of an event B is 50%?"

"No," Alan responds. "The AssurTGE Quality Director has provided us with ranges of probabilities that will help us to define the level of uncertainty of the risks. We will therefore, reason by referring to these ranges; no need to give exact probabilities. Finally ... we are not in an exact science! This makes the work easier."

Alan opens a document and displays on the screen the table below, whispering, "The probability is measured on a four-level scale."

Scale	Probability	
4	90 - 99 %	Near certainty
3	50 - 89 %	More likely
2	10 - 49 %	Less likely
1	1 - 9 %	Not likely

Table 1. Probability definition

"Do you see?" he continues. "There are scales. I let you read. For example, when we think that the probability of an event to occur is between 1 and 9 %, we will mark the risk as 'Not Likely'. When it's between 90 and 99 %, it will be considered as 'Near Certainty', and so on. Just refer to this table."

"Well, it looks simple!" Delly says. "But why would we consider an event which probability is between 1 and 9 % as 'Not Likely'? We could also say that it's 'Likely', right?"

"Absolutely!" Alan confirms. "In another company, this might be the case. This work of definition of risk scales is already done, discussed and validated by AssurTGE under the Quality Director's control. Now, projects benefit from that to qualify their risks."

He pauses and drinks a sip of water.

"Before I show you another matrix, is it clear to everyone?" he asks.

"Let me check if I've got it right," Delly responds. "I think my risk 'Inadequate support of business experts which can delay understanding of certain requirements and lead to their redevelopment' must be between 50 % and 89 % chance of happening. So, it can be marked as 'More Likely' then?"

"Referring to the matrix, that's exactly the case!" Alan confirms. "And that's what I'm going to write in front of the risk in the 'Probability' column."

"We will do the same for the impact: rate it on a scale," he continues.

Delly smiles and says:

"And the AssurTGE Quality Director has also provided you with a grid for that."

"Absolutely! And, I'm going to display it," Alan confirms.

He scrolls down a little lower in the document he had opened and shows the following table while commenting: "The impact (threat case) is measured on a scale of five levels according to the criteria defined in this matrix: Very low, Low, Moderate, High, and Very High."

Project objectives	Scales				
	Very Low	Low	Moderate	High	Very High
Cost	Overcost < 5 %	Overcost 5 % - 10 %	Overcost 10 %-20 %	Overcost 20 %-40 %	Overcost > 40 %
Time	Delay < 5 %	Delay 5 % - 10 %	Delay 10 %-20 %	Delay 20 %-40 %	Delay > 40 %
Scope	Custom labels missing but standard labels displayed	Labels and texts remain understandable by the user	Functional content affected but the result remains coherent (Excluding wording and texts)	Affected functional content giving an inconsistent result	Unusable module
Quality	Only 2 labels are impacted by use case	More than 2 labels impacted by use case	The result does not match the specified functional rules	Incoherent result display	Unusable module

Table 2. Definition of Impact Scales (case of thread)

"Here also, it's simple," he says, "I'll let you read the matrix."

He waits a few seconds, asks if the group follows him and resumes:

"We'll qualify an impact as 'Very Low', 'Low', 'Moderate', 'High' or 'Very High'. Now, the question is: When will we say that an impact is 'very Low' or 'Low'? Or takes any other value of this list?"

"Well, it's simple!" Esin responds. "The answer is in the matrix. For example, if the estimated impact is an additional cost between 10 and 20 %, we'll say that it's 'Moderate', if it exceeds 40 %, we'll say that the impact is 'Very high'."

"That's it!" Alan confirms. "But the impact can be something other than an extra cost. Do you remember the risk on the scope? If the impact on the scope is 'Unusable Module', it will be marked as 'Very High'."

"Hum," Esin says. "So, for each risk, it's necessary to evaluate the damage it would cause if it occurred?"

"Yes, exactly!" Alan responds. "And that's why you have to do it as a team with the right people to get as close as possible to a correct qualification."

The group goes through all the risks and discusses their likelihood and impact one after the other. In doing so, they qualify them. Alan fills the 'Probability' and 'Impact' columns of the risk register as the discussion progresses and writes down the extra costs when possible. Noticing that the group is distracted, he proposes a fifteen minute break.

Then, everyone goes about their own business: some make personal phone calls, others consult the messages on their smartphone or emails on their computer. Betty and Esin settle in one of the rest areas near the meeting room.

"I learn every day with my son," Betty says. "He brought me another story last night."

"Aah ... kids ... With the internet and their smartphone, they have more than a library at hand. As long as they make good use of it! So, tell, what did he tell you?" Esin asks.

"In fact, he is more and more interested in Greek mythology and tells us many of his readings at dinner."

"That's excellent, for a boy of twelve."

"Last night, he told me Europe was a Phoenician princess."

"Wait! Wait! Let's start at the beginning so that I follow you. 'Phoenician' would be to say someone from Phoenicia. But where is that?"

"It's a region roughly corresponding to current Lebanon. The Phoenicians are an ancient people from this corner. But well, we're talking about antiquity."

"OK, Europe would be a princess coming from there?"

"Yes, and according to legend, she was approached by Zeus, the supreme god of Greek mythology, and they would have had three children together."

"Oh ... yeah ...! Europe was one of Zeus's conquests then?"

"A real seducer, that Zeus, he had many conquests," Betty adds, bursting into laughter.

"So, our continent Europe is a beautiful princess?"

"Yes, that's what I learned yesterday. Do you have a five or ten-euro bill?"

"Sure, why?" Esin asks, looking surprised.

"Perfect, give me one or the other. Promise, I'll give it back to you."

Esin hands him a folded ten-euro note. Betty takes it and unfolds it. Holding it unfolded with both hands, she raises her arms and presents it in front of Esin's eyes.

"Look, do you see the beautiful Europe's face?" Betty says, smiling.

"Oh yes ... I see the beautiful princess! She's even engraved on our notes! Not bad!"

The break is over, the participants return to their place. The room is quiet and gives the impression that it's the nap time. Alan comes back, smiling.

"Well, guys, I have good news for you," he says. "For today, there's not much left to do. A few crossings of lines and columns and we're done."

All participants start to look at each other. Some are whispering words in their neighbor's ears. Others start laughing as to keep themselves awake.

"In this final stretch of our workshop," he continues, "you'll define now how much each risk is serious, or severe for the project."

"Another odd notion," Esin says.

Another adds, "We should have got right to the point, shouldn't we? Personally, all the risks I mentioned are serious." Alan laughs and says:

"You will follow the same logic as for probabilities and impacts to define the degree of severity of each risk. Some call it 'severity' of risk."

He opens again the document 'quality of AssurTGE', projects it on the screen and goes down until finding the table below:

Impact / Probability	Very High	High	Moderate	Low	Very Low
Near Certainty	Unacceptable	Unacceptable	Critical	Significant	Significant
More Likely	Unacceptable	Critical	Significant	Not significant	Not significant
Less Likely	Unacceptable	Critical	Not insignificant	Not significant	Not significant
Not Likely	Critical	Significant	Not significant	Not significant	Not significant

Table 3. Definition of risk severity

One participant says, jokingly, "Ah ... I knew there was still matrix in stock."

"In this case too," continues Alan, "you'll just have to refer to this grid to define the severity of each risk. You recognize the impact on the first line and the probability in the first column. Don't you? Just cross a line and a column and you get the severity. It's deduced simply from the probability and the impact. That's all the work that remains to do today."

"Well, for once, it could have been automated," Ethan says. "No need for a human to do that, it's a job for a machine! For each risk, when you choose the probability and the impact, the 'severity' column should fill automatically. Give me your document, and I'll complete it in two minutes. What is the next step?

"Well spotted, Ethan!" Alan says, "At the next workshop, we will review the risk response strategies and define action plans for the risks that are 'unacceptable' or 'critical'."

"And, what do we do with the others?" Ethan asks.

"They will be monitored throughout the project," Alan responds. "They will be in a list to watch. We'll talk about it again at the next workshop."

The session ends, all participants return to their office and continue their day's work.

3

It's 11:30 am. The weather is nice and mild outside. Alan opens his window slightly. He hears, faintly far in the distance, the sounds of drums mixed with cheers and shouts of joy from a crowd. *Is this the festival of music in AssurTGE or what? The employees don't care. Is that all they've got to do? Sing, dance and scream in the office while the projects spin out of control.* He decides to get close to understand what's going on. The closer he gets, the more the noise turns into energizing music.

One of the canteens overlooking the courtyard is open to the outside. Flags of a country are displayed everywhere inside and outside the canteen. They're green (vertically on the left), yellow (horizontal at the top) followed by red (horizontal at the bottom). In the courtyard, a group of men and women dressed in traditional African outfits sing and dance. The band plays African drums of different sizes, several types of bells, and many other instruments. A cheerful crowd forming a circle enjoys the show.

Suddenly a mask wearing a conical shape camouflage covered with hay emerges from a corner of the yard while dancing and turning on itself. His hays are dyed in the colors of the flags. The group accelerates the rhythm of the music. The first mask is immediately followed by a second, then a third. The group accelerates the pace by tapping more and more quickly on the bells, singing and dancing at the same time. Women chant lyrics in a foreign language as if to encourage the masks. They dance and run in the center of the circle formed by the spectators. Alan surprises his body moving to the rhythm of the music. *No, not here, you will look ridiculous. Control yourself, Alan!* Moments later, the masks arise. Some insiders remove the camouflage of a mask. There is nothing inside. It's absolutely empty! They put the camouflage back, here we go: the mask starts running and dancing again. The spectators are amazed and cheer. Alan, lost, approaches a young woman.

"Hi! Do you know what's going on?"

"Yes, I am part of the organizers. This is one of the big theme meals that AssurTGE organizes four times a year. The management regularly introduces employees to the cultures of small countries they aren't used to visiting. You must have noticed that the meals in the canteen are not European but rather African."

"Well, I've recognized the flag of the Republic of Benin. So, the dishes are also Beninese?"

"Yes, that's it. Today, we are introducing the culture of this country to our employees. At the same time, this relaxes them."

"I think it's a great idea to escape."

"In fact, the masks are called 'zangbeto'. In the culture of Benin, it seems that it means 'Guardian of the night'. They would be spirits that watch over the inhabitants in the night and chase evil spirits and the thieves."

"Oh yeah? And what will be the next culture to discover?"

"We'll change Continent. It will be another small country in Asia."

Alan's phone alarm rings. After this brief period of escape, he suddenly finds himself even more motivated to resume the course of his day's work: the spirit of 'zangheto' has undoubtedly made its effect. He strides back to his office.

2:30 pm, the workshop begins.

"Yesterday," Alan recalls, "we identified and analyzed risks. We decided to provide responses to the risks that have Severity 'Unacceptable' and 'Critical'. Well, that's what we're going to do now."

"Aaaah," cried one of the participants. "The moment I was waiting for has finally come. It's good to list the risks, but if it's just to look at them, we'll have lost all our time. Of course, we must define how to prevent them."

"Before attacking them one after the other," Alan says, "first, I'll explain the strategies and possible responses that can be made. This will inspire us."

"Wow ... Strategy! Guys, be careful of your brains. Fasten your seatbelt, that's not going to be easy," one participant says.

The room laughs.

"Well, in response to a threat or an opportunity we can ..."

Alan goes to the board and writes, "Avoid the threat or exploit the opportunity".

"This deserves an explanation!" he continues, taking a few steps towards the participants. "Yes, if it's a threat, it can be eliminated outright by simply removing its cause. In the case of an opportunity, we can completely eliminate the uncertainty associated with it."

He stops a few moments to let the group think.

"What do you mean by 'be eliminated outright?'" Alfan asks.

"For example," Alan responds, "as a consequence of the threat, to prevent it from happening, we can decide one of the following actions: remove the part of the project that could cause the risk, remove the resource that could cause risk, extend time, decrease scope, etc."

"Oh yes …!" Alfan exclaims. "Indeed, by doing so, we can eradicate the threat."

"Exactly!" Alan confirms. "On the other hand, to exploit an opportunity, we can, for example, decide to add resources or reorganize the project which increases the chance of the opportunity to occur."

Alan marks a new break, probably to retain the group's attention.

"OK, it's clear!" Alfan says.

"Another strategy is to 'Transfer the threat or share the opportunity'. In the case of a threat, we'll transfer to a third party all or part of the impact as well as the responsibility of the response."

"Obviously we won't transfer it to just anyone, I guess!" Alfan remarks.

Some participants nod to confirm Alfan's remark.

"Exactly!" Alan responds, "The third party must be able to bear the responsibility of course."

"Ah, that's what we do by taking insurance then?" Alfan asks.

"Well done Alfan! This is a good example of risk transfer. And that's also what we do by outsourcing all or part of something we have to achieve."

"OK, I understand now. But, in the case of outsourcing, don't we also take another risk?"

"Absolutely! That is why we should always do the risk analysis before signing an outsourcing contract. That way, we'll have a good knowledge of the risks induced by outsourcing and take the necessary precautions in the contract."

Participants start whispering something causing a background noise in the room. Alan stops for a moment and asks if they follow his explanations well.

Again, silence in the room. He pursues.

"In the case of an opportunity, it's the same; we give the responsibility to a third party because he is the one who has the necessary expertise to achieve what we want to do. We can for example work in partnership with him or establish any other form of collaboration but he is the one who is responsible for the response, not us."

He scans the whole room.

"Let's move on to another strategy."

"Ah, there're still other possibilities?" Alfan asks.

"Yes! Mitigate the threat or improve the opportunity. This one is very simple. For a threat, you only need to **lower** to an acceptable threshold, its probability or its impact or both at the same time. Depending on the threat, we can imagine for example to perform more tests, or make a prototype to validate a concept before going further, recruit a resource to reduce the unavailability of resources on a given expertise, etc."

"And on the other hand," he continues, "for an opportunity, by symmetry to the strategy applied to a threat, you'll just need to ..."

"Wait, wait" Gama interrupts. "Let me guess. It must be: '**increase** the probability or the impact or both at once!'".

"Great!" Alan cries. "In this case, for example, a more experienced resource can be assigned to an activity to reduce the time it takes to complete; we can take actions to increase the chance of hiring an expert, or to increase the chances of a negotiation of an expert's daily rate, etc."

Alan looks back at the other participants to try to read from their faces if they understood his explanations.

"Be careful! You must all understand the possible strategies before moving on. So far, do they seem clear to you? If not stop me, take a few moments to think about each of them."

Some answer "clear!" Others "perfect!" And others "crystal clear!"

"But, what do we do if we can't apply any of these strategies for one reason or another?" Gama asks.

"Good question," Alan replies. "This leads us straight to the last possibility: Accept the threat and the opportunity. With this strategy, whether for a threat or an opportunity, we decide to take no action until the risk occurs. However, often, a contingency plan is defined and will be followed if the risk occurs."

"Wow!" Gama exclaims. "Four response strategies. Let me recapitulate those of a threat, without looking at the board to see if I've caught everything."

"Good idea, to repeat them aloud will serve everyone," Alan says.

"Well, I recall them:"

- ✓ Avoid the risk by defining actions to eliminate it entirely. It can be for example: remove the part of the project or the resource likely to cause the risk, extend the time, reduce the scope, etc.
- ✓ Transfer the impact and the responsibility of the response to a third party; as we do when we insure ourselves against a risk.
- ✓ Mitigate it by lowering its probability or impact to an acceptable threshold or both. For example, by performing more tests, or validating a concept with a prototype, etc.
- ✓ Simply accept the risk by not taking any action until it occurs. Define a contingency plan to apply in case the risk occurs.

"You have a good memory!" Alan says, happy. "Excellent! Does anyone else want to do the same for an opportunity?"

The hubbub in the room.

"Yes, I do! I'll try," Delly says.

Silence.

"Okay, let's do it:"

- ✓ Exploit the opportunity by removing the cause of its uncertainty. For example: add resources or reorganize the project outright.
- ✓ Share with a third party the impact and the responsibility for the response. For example, we develop a partnership with a specialized third party that will achieve our work.
- ✓ Enhance the opportunity by increasing its probability or impact or both. For example, assigning a more experienced resource to an activity to complete before the scheduled end date.
- ✓ And as for a threat, simply accept the opportunity by not taking any action until the event occurs.

"Wow! You're as good as me," Gama laughs.

All the other participants burst out laughing. They comment on those strategies in a hubbub for a few moments. Alan looks at them, silent, happy to have passed his message.

"I think that deserves a break, doesn't it?" says a voice from the back of the room. "What do you think?"

Thus, the group decides on a quarter of an hour break.

As usual, Betty and Esin spend the time together. It was a nice sunny day outside, they sit in the garden.

"This weekend," Betty says, "I wandered around 'Les Champs Élysée' at night with a friend from New York visiting Paris."

"What did you do with your children?" Esin asks.

"I'm lucky for that, my parents keep them with pleasure when I need it. 'Les Champs Élysée' is beautiful, especially at night. By the way, do you know what I learned?"

"Ah ... your son again, the Greek!" Esin interrupts, laughing.

"Yes, well spotted!" Betty continues, laughing. "In Greek mythology, 'Champs Élysée' would be a part of Greek underworld where virtuous souls lived after death."

"Underworld?"

"Yes, the underworld, that is to say, the abode of the dead, all the dead without exception: the blessed, the unfortunate, and even the souls judged neither good nor bad!"

"Really?"

"Absolutely! And, the place where it was good to live, and where the blessed stayed was called 'Champs Elysées'."

"So, what's about the unfortunate people?"

"Direct to Tartarus! Yes, they were placed separately in a dark place. However, beware. In mythology, the 'unfortunate' are punished criminals! And not people who are unlucky or not happy as we could understand in our everyday language."

"I've suspected. Can you imagine? To be punished after death simply because one was unlucky during one's life? It would be a double punishment!"

"That's not all. It seems that Greeks have even reserved a separate place for souls who have accomplished nothing in their lifetime and have led a meaningless life."

"Oh, yeah?" Esin says, surprised, bursting into laughter. "So We'd better accomplish something in our lifetime then? Otherwise, we won't land at 'Champs Elysées'? Well, I'm not going to die wondering, I've learned something new today: Champs Elysées was a sweet place to live in the Greek underworld. So, I'll go there more often now ... in case I don't land there after my death because I'm still looking for what to accomplish in my lifetime."

"Hum ... 'accomplish' ... It makes me think suddenly. Leave something useful to future generations, and contribute to the endless chain of improving living conditions for humanity. That was a good point from Greeks!"

4

It's the end of the break, the workshop resumes.

"Ok," Alan begins, "the types of strategies are now clear. So they'll guide you to define our risk's responses. We'll proceed risk by risk."

"When you look at these strategies well," Alfan says, "it seems that most of the risks will only need to be mitigated. I'm talking about threats of course."

"Exactly!" Alan says, "especially since I've already explored the 'avoid', 'transfer' and 'accept' strategies. In fact, that's often the case."

Alan projects the risk register on the board. He scrolls through it, stops at a risk and reads it aloud:

"'Delay in receiving the AXM software license that could postpone the start of the management module integration leading to deliver Centragiciel v1 late.' How can we mitigate this? So, who wants to start?"

Silence. Nobody is answering. Alan thinks a few seconds and proposes the following action to initiate the movement.

"A solution is to order the licenses well in advance. This will reduce the likelihood of being delivered late."

"Yeah, that's clear, we do it early," Zely says.

"Indeed, this is already a first precaution. Another idea?" Alan asks.

"In fact," says a participant, "it takes a lot of work for suppliers to prepare these types of license. The preparation process is long. That's why delivery takes weeks or sometimes months. So, I think we have to agree with the supplier on milestones and check the progress of the license preparation."

"OK," Alan resumes, "I add: 'Agree with the supplier on milestones to check the progress of the license preparation'".

"These two actions are fine," Alan says. "But I'd add a third: 'In our contract with the supplier, include a penalty clause which provides compensation in case of delay of delivery'. This will reduce, or perhaps even cancel, the compensation we'll have to pay to our internal client if we deliver late."

"In summary, to mitigate this risk, we retain the following three actions:"

He reads aloud to the group: "

- ✓ Order licenses early enough.
- ✓ Agree with the supplier on milestones to check the progress of license preparation.

✓ In our contract with the supplier, include a penalty clause that provides compensation if we deliver late."

"Any comments?" Alan asks.

Silence.

"Perfect! Let's move on to the next," he continues.

He moves the cursor on the risk 'Inadequate support of business which can delay the understanding of certain requirements and lead to their redevelopment'.

Diane, a business representative, reacts immediately:

"For this one," I confirm, "given the work to be done, we may have a real concern for availability. I talked about it to my boss. To mitigate the risk, we will recruit an assistant for the project period; it costs 25 k €. It will help us on some of our activities, which will relieve us a bit from some works."

"OK, I write: 'Recruit an assistant to help business and increase their availability," Alan says.

He scrolls his cursor and stops on the risk 'Insufficient support from experts to developers that can delay the understanding of certain technical requirements leading to redevelop them'.

"Well, also here, we just have to hire a technical expert to assist our colleagues," Diane says.

"In the case of technical expertise," explains Alfan, "it's a bit more complicated. For all our activities, we need technical skills and a very good knowledge of our business. And it's hard to find. So, even if we had the finance, this solution wouldn't be applicable."

All participants think. Nobody talks, it's total silence for about a minute. Then, Alfan continues:

"So, I propose to plan in advance complex activities that require technical support. And to share as soon as possible technical deliverables with experts to gather their comments as soon as possible."

"OK perfect, we can also agree with them on milestones to address those technical aspects," adds Alan.

"It's also necessary to share these milestones with their line managers so that they take them into account in their overall planning," a technical representative adds.

"OK, let's summarize," Alan says: "

- ✓ Plan ahead for complex activities that require technical support.
- ✓ Share technical deliverables as soon as possible with the experts to gather their comments as soon as possible.
- ✓ Agree with experts on milestones to address technical issues.
- ✓ Share milestones with the experts' line managers"

"Any remark?" Alan asks.

He waits a few moments and displays the following risk: 'Insufficient knowledge of the specificities of the DBMS in the team which might result in writing incompatible SQL commands leading to redevelop them'.

"I discussed it with my boss and the database guys," Esin says. "We can suggest a two-day training on the specificities of our DBMS. It costs 20 k €. Compared to the time it will help us save, no problem to justify this budget!"

Alan writes: 'Plan a two-day training on the specificities of the DBMS.'

"OK, the next is," Alan says: "'Lack of inspection of legacy codes before the estimate of developments which may result in redeveloping some modules and increase project costs and time'".

"I'll save you the time!" Alfan says. "It's necessary to conduct technical studies of the existing codes before estimating the workload and share the results with the teams."

"And," Alan adds, "include the developers who participated in these studies in the workload estimates workshop."

"Perfect," Alan says, "so to summarize:"

- ✓ Conduct technical studies of the existing codes before estimating the workload and share the results with the teams
- ✓ Involve in the workload estimates workshop developers who participated in the codes studies.

The group defines the risks responses. Alan updates the 'Mitigation Plan' and 'Probability' columns in the Risk Register (see Annex 2, Table 12) as they progress.

"Wait two seconds Alan," interrupt Delly, "how do you get the values in the column 'Cost of risk?'"

"Ah ... Yes, I didn't explain it. It's simply the probability multiplied by the financial impact, I mean the extra cost. The sum of this column will give me the amount of the budget of the provisions to cover the residual risks (see an example of calculation in Annex 1, table 11) in other words those which will remain after our risk analysis.

"OK," Delly says, "but no matter how well we predict everything, there will always be risks that will have completely escaped us. Right? There may be some unexpected events, no?"

"Absolutely! For these unforeseen events, I'll discuss with Christophe and he will reserve a proportion of the budget to cover them; maybe 5% of the total budget, we'll see. It's not part of my monitoring scope."

The workshop ends and they get a table which extract is below:

Description	Action plan
Delay in receiving the AXM software license that could postpone the start of the management module integration leading to deliver Centragiciel v1 late.	✓ Order licenses early enough. ✓ Agree with the supplier on milestones to check the progress of license preparation. ✓ In our contract with the supplier, include a penalty clause that provides compensation if we deliver late."
Inadequate support of business which can delay the understanding of certain requirements and lead to their redevelopment.	Recruit an assistant to help business and increase their availability.
Insufficient support from experts to developers that can delay the understanding of certain technical requirements leading to redevelop them.	✓ Plan ahead for complex activities that require technical support. ✓ Share technical deliverables as soon as possible with the experts to gather their comments as soon as possible. ✓ Agree with experts on milestones to address technical issues. ✓ Share milestones with the experts' line managers

Table 4. Risk responses (Part 1)

Description	Action plan
Insufficient knowledge of the specificities of the DBMS in the team which might result in writing incompatible SQL commands leading to redevelop them.	Plan a two-day training on the specificities of the DBMS.
Lack of inspection of legacy codes before the estimate of developments which may result in redeveloping some modules and increase project costs and time.	✓ Conduct technical studies of the existing codes before estimating the workload and share the results with the teams. ✓ Involve in the workload estimates workshop developers who participated in the codes studies. ✓
The growing number of the module 'management' users that could lead to server overload and prevent users to access Centragiciel.	✓ Refine the requirement on the number of users. ✓ Perform performance tests taking into account the maximum number of users.

Table 5. Risk responses (Part 2)

Alan suggests that the group chooses an owner for each risk. He fills the risk register column 'Owner' as the discussions proceed.

"Thanks all, you did a great teamwork," he says. "First, you've identified our project's risks. Then you analyzed them. Finally, you have provided preventative responses to those who need it. Well, our workshop on risk ends at this stage."

He drinks a sip of water and continues.

"As you can imagine, we will implement these preventive actions throughout the project. In addition, every week, we'll re-evaluate all risks and identify new ones. Do you see? A real risk monitoring work still lies ahead of us."

Alfan, proud of the work accomplished, also probably happy that the workshop ends, gets up, fist raised and chants: "Yeah ... the risk fishing has just started!" All his other colleagues follow him and respond all together: "and it will last the whole project lifetime!"

Alan bursts out laughing and exclaims, "Wow, you're very enthusiastic!"

That concludes the meeting. The whole group gets around the coffee machine, discusses a moment, and progressively disperses.

Section 2: Annexes

Annex 1 – Risks Management Plan

1 Risk Management Plan

A risk is an uncertain event or condition that, if it occurs, has a positive or negative effect on one or more project objectives such as scope, schedule, cost and quality.

The project manager and his team will follow the process defined in this paragraph to manage AlfaProject's risks.

1.1 Methodology

The steps to follow are described below:

Step 1: Identify the risks

For each workpackage of the WBS, the project manager will determine the risks for each of the categories listed in the § 1.5. He will complete his research by analyzing the assumptions and constraints using the table 6 below, questioning experts and consulting the list of risks encountered in previous projects. The final list must be approved in a risk review session before moving to the next step.

Hypothesis or Constraints	Could this hypothesis or constraint be false? (Yes/No)	If the hypothesis or the constraint is false, would this impact the project? (Yes/No)	Does it lead to a risk?

Table 6. Example: assumptions and constraints analysis.

When a hypothesis or a constraint leads to risk, describe the risk according to the template: "statement of the assumption/constraint" can reveal false and leads to "statement of the consequence on the objective of the project".

At the end of this step, the following fields of the risk register might have been filled:

- ✓ Title
- ✓ Description
- ✓ Causes (if already known)
- ✓ Responses (if already known)
- ✓ Planned date of the response (if already known)

Step 2: Analyze the risks

The project manager will follow the actions below to analyze the risks identified in the previous step:

- ✓ For each risk, determine the likelihood and impact according to scales defined in the tables 7 and 8 below.
- ✓ Determine the severity: unacceptable, critical, significant and Not significant by referring to the table 9
- ✓ Decide the risks that need a response

The probability is measured on a scale of 4 levels:

Level	Probability	
4	90 - 99 %	Near certainty
3	50 - 89 %	More likely
2	10 - 49 %	Less likely
1	1 - 9 %	Not likely

Table 7. Probability definition

The impact (case of threat) is measured on a scale of 5 levels as defined in the table 8 below: Very low, Low, Moderate, High and Very high.

Project objectives	Scales of impact				
	Very Low	Low	Moderate	High	Very High
Cost	Overcost < 5 %	Overcost 5 % - 10 %	Overcost 10 % - 20 %	Overcost 20 % - 40 %	Overcost > 40 %
Time	Delay < 5 %	Delay 5 % - 10 %	Delay 10 % - 20 %	Delay 20 % - 40 %	Delay > 40 %
Scope	Custom labels are missing but standard labels are displayed	Labels and texts remain understandable by the user	Functional content impacted but the result remains coherent (Excluding wording and texts)	Functional content impacted and the result is inconsistent	The module is unusable
Quality	Only 2 labels are impacted by the use case	More than 2 labels are impacted by the use case	The result does not match the specified functional rules	Incoherent result is displayed	The module is unusable

Table 8. Definition of Impact Scales (case of threat)

Impact / Probability	Very High	High	Moderate	Low	Very Low
Near Certainty	Unacceptable	Unacceptable	Critical	Significant	Significant
More Likely	Unacceptable	Critical	Significant	Not significant	Not significant
Less Likely	Unacceptable	Critical	Significant	Not significant	Not significant
Not Likely	Critical	Significant	Not significant	Not significant	Not significant

Table 9. Definition of risk severity

Step 3: Plan risk responses

The project manager will create a working group composed of members of the project team and any other stakeholder that can bring its expertise to find a solution to the risks. To prepare the workshops, he will assign the risk to participants based on their competence and expertise. They will do the actions listed below:

For each of the risks decided in the previous step,

- ✓ Study the responses proposed in step 1 and deepen them
- ✓ Define options if necessary
- ✓ Choose an option (contingency plan)
- ✓ Determine the secondary risks (risks caused by the implementation of the response)
- ✓ Determine residual risks (risks remained after the implementation of the response)
- ✓ Define the actions to take in case the contingency plan turns out to be inadequate (fallback plan)
- ✓ Describe the triggers which will help to know when to start the execution of the contingency plan
- ✓ Assign an owner for the risk: the owner will have the responsibility to monitor the triggers and give the "go" for the execution of the action plan when the conditions are met. He is responsible for the implementation of the response plan.
- ✓ Define the budget and the schedule of the activities related to the responses.

If the risk response plan changes at least one objective of the project, the change must be approved in accordance with the change management plan process described in § 3 Change Management Plan.

Participants can refer to the response's strategies below:

Thread:

- ✓ Avoid the risk by defining actions to eliminate it entirely. It can be for example: remove the part of the project or the resource likely to cause the risk, extend the time, reduce the scope, etc.
- ✓ Transfer the impact and the responsibility of the response to a third party (as we do when we buy insurance).
- ✓ Mitigate it by lowering its probability or impact to an acceptable threshold or both. For example, by performing more tests, or validating a concept with a prototype, etc.
- ✓ Simply accept the risk by not taking any action until it occurs. Define a contingency plan to apply in case the risk occurs.

Opportunity:

- ✓ Exploit the opportunity by removing the cause of its uncertainty. For example: add resources or reorganize the project outright.
- ✓ Share with a third party the impact and the responsibility of the response. For example, develop a partnership with a specialized third party that will achieve our work.
- ✓ Enhance the opportunity by increasing its probability or impact or both. For example,

assigning a more experienced resource to an activity to complete it before the planned end date.
- ✓ And as for a threat, simply accept the opportunity by not taking any action until the event occurs.

Step 4: Monitor and control the risks: Assess the result of the action plan execution

The project manager should ensure the application of the actions below during the project lifecycle:

- ✓ Monitor the risk triggers
- ✓ Implement the action plans and control their application
- ✓ Reassess the risks
- ✓ Identify new risks and manage them by following the process described in this paragraph
- ✓ Communicate on risks, example: number of risks occurred last month, Effectiveness of the responses, status of current risk responses, number of risks that will potentially occur the next month and the provisions planned to manage them.
- ✓ Improve the risk management process when necessary
- ✓ Compare remaining risk budget to the project risks and check if they are sufficient to cover all the project risks.

1.2 Roles and responsibilities (in risk management process)

All stakeholders are likely to participate in the risk management process, including those outside the project team. The table below provides only the main actors.

Roles	Responsibilities
Project Manager	✓ Manages all the stages of the risk management process ✓ Develops the risk response plan ✓ Presents the response plan to steering committee members ✓ Updates the project management plan, the risk register and any other documents related to the risk management process.
Project Committee	Participates in all stages of the risk management process.
Steering Committee	✓ Approves the risk response plans when required ✓ Allocates the resources required for the implementation of the response plans.

Table 10. Roles and responsibilities

1.3 Budget (extract of calculation example)

Risk description	Consequence	Probability	Calculation of provisions (Time)	Calculation of provisions (Cost)
Delay in receiving the AXM software license that could postpone the start of the management module integration leading to deliver Centragiciel v1 late.	✓ Cost increase of 150 k€ ✓ Time: 2 weeks delay (10 days)	40 %	10 days x 40 % = 4 days	150 k€ x 40 % => + 60 k€ (Increase)
Renegotiation of pricing conditions with our provider People2YourC that could lower the current daily rate and reduce the team cost.	Cost: decrease of 20 k€	60 %		20 k€ x 60 % => -12 k€ (Decrease)
The internal IT department will probably move many workstations this year; which will slow down developments if this is done	✓ Cost: increase of 200 k€ ✓ Time: a week delay (5 days)	20 %	5 days x 20 % = 1 day	200 k€ x 20 % => + 40 k€ (Increase)
Total Provisions			5 days (4 + 1)	+ 88 k€ (+ 60-12 + 40)

Table 11. Example: Cost of risk calculation

1.4 Risk review schedule

The risk review will be done every week. In addition to this frequency, when necessary, the project manager can schedule a specific workshop to review the risks.

1.5 Risk categories

The initial list of categories below will help to explore the sources of risk. It must be updated throughout the project lifecycle:

- ✓ Definition of needs
- ✓ Quality
- ✓ Resources
- ✓ Time
- ✓ Technology
- ✓ Application of the project management plan recommendations
- ✓ Assumptions
- ✓ Dependency
- **Sponsor and stakeholders Involvement**

Annex 2 – Risks monitoring

NO.	Identification			Qualification				Follow-up	Treatment		
	Risk	Consequence	Cost of risk	Date of identification	Probability	Forecast date when the risk could occur	Impact level	Severity	Status	Risk response action plan	Owner of the risk	Action date
1												
2												
3												
4												
5												
6												
7												
8												
9												
10												
11												
12												
13												

Table 12. Risks monitoring

Bibliography and Internet References

Projects

- ✓ A Guide to the Project Management Body of Knowledge (PMBOK Guide) Sixth Edition
- ✓ Rita Mulcahy's PMP Exam Prep, Seventh Edition
- ✓ Mike Griffiths, PMI-ACP Exam Pep Second Edition

Anecdotes

- ✓ http://www.sciencesetavenir.fr/Espace/astrophysique/ondes-gravitationnelles-comment-la-collision-de-2-trous-noirs-fait-vibrer-l-univers_23389
- ✓ http://dailygeekshow.com/Mythologie-grece-anecdotes/
- ✓ http://www.pheniciens.com/articles/Decouverte.php

www.ingramcontent.com/pod-product-compliance
Lightning Source LLC
Chambersburg PA
CBHW030952240526
45463CB00016B/2523